TEAM NINJA

Written by Catherine Saunders

DK

LONDON, NEW YORK, MUNICH,
MELBOURNE and DELHI

Editor Rosie Peet
Designers Jenny Edwards, Stefan Georgiou, and Jon Hall
Pre-Production Producer Siu Yin Chan
Producer Louise Daly
Managing Editor Paula Regan
Managing Art Editor Guy Harvey
Art Director Lisa Lanzarini
Publisher Julie Ferris
Publishing Director Simon Beecroft

Designed for DK by Rich T Media

Reading Consultant Linda B. Gambrell, Ph.D

Dorling Kindersley would like to thank Randi Sorensen, Paul Hansford
and Martin Leighton at the LEGO Group.

First American edition, 2016
Published in the United States by DK Publishing
345 Hudson Street, New York, New York 10014

Page design copyright © 2016 Dorling Kindersley Limited
DK, a Division of Penguin Random House LLC
16 17 18 19 20 10 9 8 7 6 5 4 3 2 1
001–290560–Jul/2016

A catalog record for this book is available from the Library of Congress.
ISBN: 978-1-4654-5192-7 (Hardback)
ISBN: 978-1-4654-5191-0 (Paperback)

DK books are available at special discounts when purchased in
bulk for sales promotions, premiums, fund-raising, or educational use.
For details, contact: DK Publishing Special Markets,
345 Hudson Street, New York, New York 10014
SpecialSales@dk.com

Printed and bound in China

www.LEGO.com

www.dk.com

A WORLD OF IDEAS:
SEE ALL THERE IS TO KNOW

Contents

Meet the Ninja!

Ninjago Island is a beautiful place, where adventure, mystery, and danger are never far away. According to legend, this world was created many thousands of years ago by the First Spinjitzu Master. He used the combined energy of the Four Golden Weapons—the Sword of Fire, the Shurikens of Ice, the Scythe of Quakes, and the Nunchuks of Lightning.

Ninjago Island is a special place, and many evildoers have sought to take control of it. So far,

Cole

Zane

Nya

they have all failed, thanks to a team of highly skilled ninja. These special ninja use an ancient martial art known as Spinjitzu to keep their land safe. Spinjitzu Masters can become a tornado of energy by spinning very quickly. Today, the Ninjago world is under the protection of six Spinjitzu Masters—Cole, Zane, Nya, Lloyd, Kai, and Jay. They were trained by the wise Master Wu. Come and meet them!

Jay

Kai

Lloyd

Jay, the Lightning Ninja, can use the power of lightning to create a tornado of electricity when he spins. Like his element, Jay is fast, powerful, and extremely bright. He can leap into battle as quick as a flash and wield two weapons at once. He has a flair for inventing, too.

When Jay was first spotted by Master Wu, he was testing out one of his inventions—a pair of mechanical wings. The wings didn't work, but Wu realized that Jay was special and would be a great ninja. Jay is proud to be a ninja and trains hard every day. He also uses his inventing skills to make sure that the ninja's vehicles are equipped with the latest technology.

Jay has a great sense of humor. Well, at least he thinks so—his fellow ninja don't always find his jokes so funny! Jay also has a crush on his teammate Nya.

When Kai the
Fire Ninja spins, he
becomes a tornado
of fire, sizzling with
energy. Kai has
always had a
connection with
fire, because his
father was a
blacksmith. Kai and
his sister, Nya,
inherited the family

business from him. Kai was happy being a
blacksmith and especially enjoyed making swords.
However, Master Wu saw that Kai had the
potential to become a great ninja. Now, Kai is a
powerful ninja. Swords remain his favorite ninja
weapons, and he and Nya can still make new
swords for the team in their blacksmith's shop.

Sometimes, Kai's personality is as fiery as his
element. He can be hot-headed, impatient, and
stubborn. Although Kai works hard to control
his emotions, he will leap into action without
thinking about the consequences if the people
he loves are in trouble.

Nya, the Water Ninja, is Kai's little sister and the newest member of the ninja team. She can spin swirling whirlpools, generate powerful tidal waves, and control the water inside objects.

For a long time, people only saw Nya as Kai's little sister. Nya was determined to show everyone that she could be a great warrior, too, so she designed her own armor and equipment and became the mysterious hero Samurai X. When the ninja learned Samurai X's true identity, they were impressed. Master Wu asked Nya to join the ninja. At first she wasn't sure it was right for her, but she learned that with training she could become the Water Ninja.

Nya is a brave ninja. As the only girl, she is eager to prove that she's just as good as the boys. She's a whizz on a Ninja Bike, and she's set her sights on beating all her older brother Kai's training records!

These days, Lloyd is the Green Ninja, Master of Energy, but he wasn't always such a hero. When he was younger, all Lloyd wanted to do was impress his father, the evil Lord Garmadon. So Lloyd enrolled in Darkley's School for Bad Boys and tried to learn how to be evil. However, Lloyd was expelled from the school for not being evil enough. Later, with the help of his uncle, Master Wu, Lloyd realized that his true destiny was to become the legendary Green Ninja. After training hard with Master Wu, Lloyd was ready to join the team.

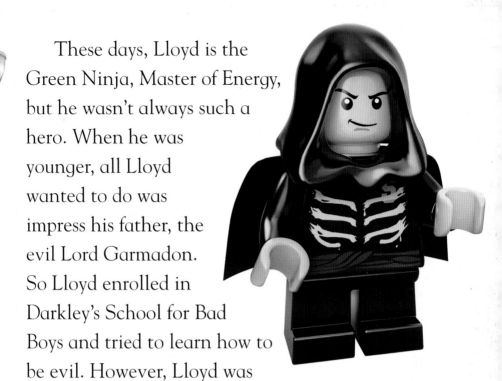

As the Green Ninja, Lloyd is very special, and he is good at lots of things. He is a skilled fighter and can wield many different weapons. He is also able to summon up a Green Energy Dragon, which shoots blasts of energy from its mouth and flies Lloyd anywhere he needs to go. Lloyd takes being a ninja very seriously and always focuses on what's best for the team.

Cole was climbing the highest mountain on Ninjago Island when Master Wu spotted his potential. Strong, tough, and determined, Cole has become a mighty ninja. He's a calm leader and a loyal friend who always puts his team first. As the Earth Ninja, Cole can spin dirt and soil into powerful tornados and create earth-splitting quakes that make his enemies tremble with fear.

Cole is the ultimate tough guy, and he is practically fearless. He is also very graceful and agile, thanks to all the dance lessons he took when he was a child.

Life was good for Cole until he got trapped in a haunted temple and turned into a ghost. At first, Cole was pretty spooked and found it difficult to adapt to his new ghostly form. However, he has discovered that he has some cool new powers as a result, such as the ability to pass through walls. Now he can't wait to freak out his foes!

Cool, calm, and always in control, Zane is the very focused Ice Ninja. When he spins, he creates tornados of ice and snow. Zane's favorite weapon is a shuriken, also known as a throwing star, which he can use with deadly accuracy. He is a little unusual—Master Wu found him meditating at the bottom of a frozen pond—but the other ninja love his strange ways.

For many years Zane couldn't remember much about his early life. He had no idea who his parents were, so the ninja became his family. However, one day Zane learned the truth—he's a robot, or "Nindroid," created by a scientist named Dr. Julien. At first Zane was shocked to learn that he was different, but his ninja family helped him realize that it didn't matter. Zane is clever, loyal, and a dedicated ninja—that's what counts. Plus, because he is a Nindroid, if Zane gets injured, he can be rebuilt and rebooted. Cool!

Wu is the youngest son of the First Spinjitzu Master, founder of the Ninjago world. He has spent his life trying to continue his father's work and keep Ninjago Island safe and peaceful. Wu is a powerful Spinjitzu Master, with many advanced skills, but his favorite weapon is still a good, old-fashioned staff, which he wields with speed and accuracy.

For many years, Wu worked alone, but as the forces of evil grew stronger, he realized that he needed help. So Wu traveled the land looking for the strongest, quickest, bravest, and cleverest people to train as ninja. First he found Cole, then Jay, then Zane, and finally Kai. Later, Wu's nephew, Lloyd, and Kai's sister, Nya, joined to complete the team.

Wu is a wise, calm, and patient man. He has been on many amazing adventures and battled many fearsome foes, but he is happiest when Ninjago Island is at peace and he can spend his days quietly drinking tea.

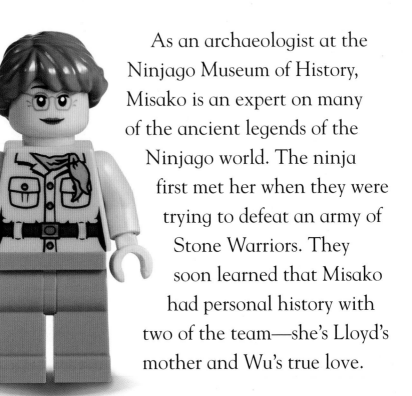

As an archaeologist at the Ninjago Museum of History, Misako is an expert on many of the ancient legends of the Ninjago world. The ninja first met her when they were trying to defeat an army of Stone Warriors. They soon learned that Misako had personal history with two of the team—she's Lloyd's mother and Wu's true love.

Many years ago, Misako chose to marry Wu's brother, Garmadon, instead of Wu. She always felt that she had made the wrong choice, so when she met Wu again, she decided she would go with him and help him train the next generation of ninja.

Misako and Wu are a great team. Misako is also a wise and patient teacher, and she is glad to have the opportunity to get to know her son better. She is very proud of Lloyd. Misako also likes to take care of Nya. She encourages the new ninja to be herself and find her own strengths, rather than copying Kai and the others.

Ninja Training

When Wu met the team, he saw their potential, but knew it would take hard work to turn them into skilled ninja. Becoming a ninja isn't easy: ninja must be strong and able to handle many different weapons. They must also be quick, agile, and able to move stealthily without their enemies spotting them, and, of course, they must master Spinjitzu.

Wu likes to send his trainees all over Ninjago Island to test their skills. The Mountain Shrine is perched high in the mountains and is the perfect place for Kai to practice his Spinjitzu. Cole prefers the Ninja Training Outpost in the jungle for practicing using different weapons.

Master Wu doesn't just train the ninja's bodies, he trains their minds, too. Ninja must be wise, patient, and able to work together, in any location.

WU'S TRAINING TIPS

I am proud of my pupils, but being a ninja is a tough job. We train every day so that we are ready for whatever—or whoever—our next challenge may be. I believe that there are five important parts of ninja training.

ACTIVITY	TIME	STAR STUDENT
1. Fitness—a ninja must be strong and fit, so my team runs every morning. My exercise program builds strength, balance, and flexibility.	**2 hours** per day	Cole is the strongest ninja and often volunteers to do extra training.
2. Weapons training—a ninja needs to master many weapons, such as swords, axes, daggers, and shurikens. It takes time to learn how to use each weapon safely and skilfully.	**1-2 hours** per day	Jay can wield two weapons as easily as one.
3. Combat skills—a ninja must learn the art of stealth and be ready for battle. Members of the team practice battling each other so that they are ready for their next foe.	**2-3 hours** per day	Kai is a brave fighter who never gives up.
4. Spinjitzu—when a ninja first learns Spinjitzu, it can make him or her feel dizzy. It's important to practice every day to get used to the spinning motion.	**30 minutes** per day	Nya is my newest recruit, but she mastered Spinjitzu very quickly.
5. In the mind—training a ninja's body is not enough—the mind must also be ready. A ninja must be patient and learn to think before leaping into battle.	**2-3 hours** meditation per day	Zane and Lloyd are the calmest and wisest members of the team.

Kai proves his **combat skills** by swinging on a rope from a treetop hiding place.

Zane creates a tornado of ice as he practices the art of **Spinjitzu**.

These ghostly foes are no match for Nya with a dagger as she puts her **weapons training** into practice.

At first Cole didn't see what he could learn from **resting** and **drinking tea**. But Wu showed him that a true ninja must also be **calm, patient,** and **wise**.

The Spinjitzu dojo is a large space for the ninja to practice the art of Spinjitzu safely. The thick walls are tough enough to withstand tornados of fire, ice, earth, or lightning. The Spinjitzu dojo is the perfect place for the ninja to develop their skills. Not only does it look cool, but it also contains all of their favorite weapons—axes, swords, spears, and shurikens.

Wu designed the dojo himself, and it has many special features to help the ninja learn to move and think quickly. Obstacles, traps,

and other surprises mean that they never know
what to expect, so they must be ready for anything.
Watch out for falling axes, spinning swords,
flaming pits, snake surprises, and booby traps!

The ninja are always eager to learn new skills. It's very important to keep one step ahead of their enemies—plus, training is fun! The ninja have mastered the art of Spinjitzu, but now they face a new challenge—Airjitzu.

Created by the mysterious Master Yang, Airjitzu is an awesome martial art. Like Spinjitzu, Airjitzu allows the ninja to create tornados, but this time they can use them to fly!

A scroll at the Temple of Airjitzu contains the secret of this special martial art. The creepy temple is haunted by the ghost of Master Yang, but the team are determined to learn the secret of Airjitzu, so they travel to the temple to find the scroll.

The team's bravery pays off. They manage to retrieve the scroll and learn all about Airjitzu. But Cole gets a little more than he planned for, when a run-in with Master Yang turns him into a ghost!

Ninja Gear

The ninja never know what kind of enemy they might face next. They must be ready for anyone or anything, so they are experts in the use of many different types of weapons. However, each ninja has a favorite weapon—Kai likes swords, while Jay prefers nunchucks; Cole is great with a scythe, and Zane is skilled with shurikens; Nya favors a trident, while Lloyd likes to be prepared and always has a spare sword handy.

Sometimes it takes a special weapon to defeat a particular foe. For example, the team used the high-tech Techno-Blades to defeat the Overlord. When the team faced an army of Ghost Warriors, their usual weapons were useless against their phantom foes. Luckily, they obtained some Aeroblades and were soon able to slice through the spooks. Perhaps the most unusual ninja weapons are the Jade Blades, which they used in a competition called the Tournament of Elements.

The Ninjago world was built using the power of four main elements—fire, ice, earth, and lightning—and each element is linked to a powerful Golden Weapon. Often wielded by Kai, the flaming Sword of Fire can shoot fireballs and become a blade cycle, while the Shurikens of Ice can freeze anything they hit, shoot ice beams, and transform into Zane's snowmobile. The mighty Scythe of Quakes can create earthquakes, cut stone, and, when used by Cole, turn into a tread

Sword of Fire

Nunchuks of Lightning

assault vehicle. Last but not least, the Nunchuks of Lightning—Jay's favorite weapon—can create powerful energy, shoot lightning, and transform into a storm fighter jet.

The weapons were all made by the First Spinjitzu Master, who left them to his sons, Wu and Garmadon. Over the years, many have plotted to steal the weapons, but the ninja have always kept them safe. When joined together, the Golden Weapons form one awesome Mega Weapon.

Scythe of Quakes

Shurikens of Ice

When their usual weapons aren't quite enough to defeat their enemies, the ninja can harness the awesome fighting power of their robot mechs. Huge but surprisingly agile, the mechs have enough weapons to make any sensible enemy run away as fast as they can.

It takes practice to learn how to operate all the different parts of a mech at the same time, but the ninja are experts. Each mech has space for one ninja in the cockpit, and Cole's Earth Mech can be combined with Jay's Lightning Offroader to create a super vehicle called the Thunder Raider.

When the team faced an almost indestructible Stone Army, commanded by Garmadon, they had to try to wipe them out. Thanks to Kai's Fire Mech and the ultimate ninja weapon—the ancient Golden Mech, they were able to defeat the Stone Army. Piloted by Lloyd, the Golden Mech can also fly—it has rocket boosters in its feet.

There are many dragons on Ninjago Island. These enormous creatures look terrifying but, like the ninja, they just want to protect Ninjago Island. Before the ninja found them, the Ice, Fire, Lightning, and Earth Dragons each guarded one of the four Golden Weapons. They wanted to prevent the Golden Weapons from falling into Lord Garmadon's hands.

As part of their path to becoming true ninja, each trainee must tame their dragon to achieve DX (Dragon eXtreme) status. Zane, Kai, Jay, and Cole tamed the Ice, Fire, Lightning, and Earth Dragons, and now they can ride them.

The Ice, Fire, Lightning, and Earth Dragons can join together to form one four-headed Ultra Dragon. Only Green Ninja Lloyd is able to ride the Ultra Dragon.

After a lot of training, the ninja are able to summon Elemental Dragons. These mysterious beasts only appear if a ninja clears his or her mind of fear, which takes a lot of skill and discipline.

DRAGONS

These dragons may look scary, but once the ninja earn their trust, they are great allies. Some dragons protect special weapons, while others can be summoned by the ninja at will.

ICE DRAGON

The ninja found the Ice Dragon in the Frozen Wasteland, where it was guarding the Shurikens of Ice. It can breathe ice and has icicle-sharp claws.

FIRE DRAGON

When Kai tamed the Fire Dragon, he named it Flame. This dragon can shoot fire from its mouth, and it has a single flame on the end of its tail.

EARTH DRAGON

When the Earth Dragon stomps its legs, the ground shakes! It can also knock out enemies by thrashing its tail from side to side.

LIGHTING DRAGON

The Lightning Dragon was given the job of guarding the Nunchuks of Lightning. This dragon is the only one of the ninja's dragons that has six limbs.

ULTRA DRAGON

When the Ice, Fire, Earth, and Lightning Dragons were molting, they joined together to form one four-headed Ultra Dragon. Only Lloyd can ride this dragon.

GOLDEN DRAGON

When Lloyd became the Ultimate Spinjitzu Master, he gained the power to summon the mighty Golden Dragon.

ELEMENTAL DRAGON

If a ninja has conquered his or her fears, he or she can summon an Elemental Dragon. Jay's Elemental Dragon crackles with lightning.

The ninja need a range of different vehicles so that whatever their next mission is, they are always ready to go. The team has vehicles to suit any mission and, thanks to Jay and Nya's engineering skills, they are all equipped with the latest gadgets and weapons.

One of Cole's favorite vehicles is his Blaster Bike. It has rotating rapid-fire shooters that launch missiles at enemies, and its two huge wheels can navigate the rockiest of terrain.

Jay's favorite vehicle, the Jay Walker One, is specially equipped to fight ghosts. It has a disk shooter, a cannon that shoots lightning, and even

a special compartment
at the back where
captured ghouls can be
locked away.

Cool, calm Zane
prefers to simply glide
into the action. His
one-person glider is so
cool that it trails ice in its wake. It has blades
and swords on the sides that can flick out and
pierce any enemy aircraft
that come near.

What a ninja wears is very important. The uniform must feel comfortable, allow a range of movements, and be tough enough to survive fierce battles. The basic outfit consists of a ninja jacket, lightweight pants, and a special belt. The Ninja often wear a hood and a mask to protect their faces and conceal their true identities.

Ninja uniforms can be any color, but the ninja like to show off their elemental colors on their suits. Kai's is a fiery red, Jay's an electric blue, Cole's an earthy black, and Zane's a cool white. Lloyd used to wear a gold uniform when he was the Golden Ninja, but nowadays he wears his Green Ninja suit. Now that Nya has joined the team, she wears a dark red suit, with a blue mask and belt to represent her element, water. The team sometimes adapt their uniforms, adding special armor when they are practicing Kendo, or proudly displaying dragon symbols when they acheive DX status. When the team mastered Airjitzu, they got special uniforms to show off their new skill.

Ninjago Island

Ninjago Island is a fascinating place, with lots of interesting things to see and do. Nature lovers can take a trip to the Golden Peaks or the Forest of Tranquility, history fans can check out the Floating Ruins, and eager explorers can venture into the Toxic Bogs— if they dare! But everyone should take the time to visit the capital, Ninjago City. It's a fun, lively place and the island's largest city.

Ninjago City boasts lots of cool places to visit, such as the Ninjago Museum of History, where Misako used to work; the Aquarium, which features several rare species of shark; and the Concert Hall, which hosts the annual Ninjago Talent show. It also features lots of interesting buildings, from modern skyscrapers, such as the Borg Tower, to ancient wonders, such as the Ninjago Temple.

Ninjago Island's hottest spot is the Fire Temple. Deep in the Forest of Tranquility, it sits atop an active volcano, which can reach temperatures of more than 1800°F. Master Wu thought this would be the perfect place to hide the Sword of Fire from his brother, Lord Garmadon, and he asked the Fire Dragon to guard it.

Unfortunately, Lord Garmadon found the sword. However, he needed help from the Master of Fire, Kai, to steal it. Of course, Kai wasn't about to help such an evil person steal a powerful

Golden Weapon, so Garmadon kidnapped Kai's sister, Nya, and took her to the Fire Temple. Then, Kai had no choice but to use the sword to free her.

Kai managed to free his sister, but then they came face to face with the Fire Dragon! Most other people would have been fried, but Kai is the Fire Ninja. He tamed the dragon and named it Flame. Master Wu was then able to save the sword from his brother's evil clutches.

The Wailing Alps are Ninjago Island's highest point. They get their name from the sound that the wind makes as it gusts past the snowy peaks. Covered in snow and ice, the Wailing Alps are cold, steep, and very dangerous. Legend has it that the tomb of the evil Hyponbrai serpents is located here, safely buried underneath layers of snow.

Few people have ever dared to climb the Wailing Alps. However, when the ninja needed

to get to the Cloud Kingdom, they had no choice—
the only way to get there was via the mountains.

The ninja feared that the strong winds would
blow them right off the mountains, so they used
their robot mechs to scale the snowy peaks. The
plan worked and they made it to the top safely,
passing the mysterious Hanging Temple.

No one knows for sure how high the mountains
are, but Zane estimates that they must be at least
10 miles (16 km) high!

Stiix was once a bustling fishing city, but since becoming possessed by the evil spirit, Morro, it is now home to some of Ninjago Island's scariest villains. The city is built on the Endless Ocean so it is also home to some scary sea creatures, including a seaweed monster. Visiting Stiix is definitely not recommended!

Unfortunately, the ninja's quest for the Scroll of Airjitzu led them to Stiix. Surely the creepy inhabitants would be no match for the mighty ninja? The team traveled to the city in Nya's speedboat. As they got closer to Stiix, a ghostly shooter took aim at them from a rooftop. The team managed to dock safely, but they soon got caught up in the shady world of Stiix. After trying to acquire the Scroll honestly, the team realized that the only way to get their hands on it would be to steal it!

STIIX

The city of Stiix is scary enough during the day since Morro possessed it, but it is even spookier at night. Ghosts lurk around every corner, and the whole place is riddled with sneaky traps. Only a ninja would be brave enough to visit this ghostly city!

Frightening Foes

As a child, Garmadon was a ninja-in-training with his younger brother, Wu. However, a bite from a serpent, the Great Devourer, transformed him into the wicked Lord Garmadon, whose eyes glow red with evil. To protect Ninjago Island, Wu defeated his brother in a duel and sent him to the spooky Underworld.

Unfortunately, the Underworld was the perfect place for Garmadon to find some evil helpers. First, with the help of the Skeleton Army, he tried to take the Golden Weapons, but the ninja defeated him. Then, he joined forces with the slimy Serpentine, but the ninja won that battle, too. Finally, Garmadon took control of the Stone Army alongside the Overlord. But his evil plan took a different turn—Garmadon's son, Lloyd, defeated the Overlord, turning his father back into a good person.

Garmadon was so happy to be reunited with his brother, Wu, and his son, Lloyd, that he became a loyal friend of the ninja. He started to help the ninja, instead of fighting against them.

The five Serpentine tribes used to rule Ninjago Island, but the sneaky snakes could never agree on anything. The people of Ninjago got so tired of their squabbles that they captured them and locked them in separate tombs. However, many years later young Lloyd Garmadon accidentally set the Serpentine free—and they were determined to take control of the island once more.

The Serpentine wield many different weapons, but each tribe has a special power. Anyone bitten by a member of the Venomari tribe, such as Spitta,

Pythor

Spitta

Skales

imagines that their greatest fear has come to life. A bite from General Fangtom or one of his Fangpyres turns the victim into a snake. The Constrictai, led by Skalidor, squeeze all the air out of their victims, while anyone who looks General Skales and the Hypnobrai in the eyes will fall under their hypnotic spell. However, the worst Serpentine of all is the Great Devourer. This huge serpent just eats anyone who gets in his way, such as Pythor, the last member of the ancient Anacondrai tribe.

Skalidor

Fangtom

The Underworld is the home of the Skulkins, or Skeleton Army, a battalion of bony bad guys who are determined to beat the ninja. Like the ninja, the Skulkins use the power of the elements, but they use it for evil!

Samukai is the General of Fire and he can wield four weapons at once, thanks to his four arms. General of Earth, Kruncha, is strong and fierce and always wears his battle helmet. One-eyed Nuckal is the most fun of the Skulkin

generals, but he is not very smart. Wyplash is the General of Ice, and this cool commander is always thinking up clever battle plans.

Before he turned good, Lord Garmadon used to lead the Skeleton Army, with General Samukai as his second-in-command. Other spooky Skulkins include the wacky warrior Krazi, ferocious Frakjaw, and chilling Chopov. Brilliant Bonezai designs their vehicles, including the weapons-laden Skull Truck and the speedy Skull Motorbike.

When the scientist Dr. Julien created his first Nindroid, he had good intentions. He wanted to make an intelligent, human-like robot, and he was very proud of the result: Zane. However, when the evil Overlord acquired Dr. Julien's robot plans, he had a very different idea—he created an army of robots programmed to carry out his evil plans.

The new Nindroids had more advanced programming than Zane, making them faster and stronger than him. However, while Zane makes his own decisions, the new Nindroids obeyed their master without question.

Once, the Nindroid Army captured Master Wu and turned him into an evil robot named Techno Wu. When the ninja tried to steal the Overlord's special weapons, the Techno-Blades, Techno Wu chased them on a mechanical MechDragon. Luckily, the ninja were able to escape with the Techno-Blades. They used the high-tech weapons to defeat the Overlord and his Nindroids, restoring Master Wu to his old self.

NINJAGO CITY

YOUR DAILY NEWSPAPER SERVING THE NINJAGO COMMUNITY

NEWS

NOBLE NINJA NAB NASTY NINDROIDS

Today the people of Ninjago Island can rest easy because, once again, the brave ninja have saved us all. When an army of rogue robots attacked Ninjago City, our fate seemed sealed, but a team of mighty heroes came to our rescue, just in time.

The battle for control of our beloved city centered on the ancient Ninjago Temple. The marauding machines attacked the sacred site with laser cannons, but the ninja fought back using the Temple's catapult and secret disk shooter.

BATTLING BLUE NINJA BASHES BOT

Jay, Master of Lightning, is shown here in the middle of a fierce battle with a Nindroid. The mean machine is no match for the ninja's glowing weapon, which secret sources have revealed is known as a Techno Blade.

MESSED-UP MASTERMIND

Latest reports suggest that the Nindroids were programmed by this sinister figure, last seen during the Stone Army's failed invasion. Known as the Overlord, he was widely believed to have been destroyed. Now, rumor has it that he has been restored as a powerful digital version.

The Stone Army is one of the ninja's most ancient foes. Created by the mysterious Overlord, it was originally defeated by the First Spinjitzu Master, who buried it under Ninjago City. However, years later the sneaky Serpentine managed to unearth the army and evil Lord Garmadon took control of it.

Led by General Kozu, the Stone Army is made of indestructible Dark Materials, making it a pretty tough enemy to beat! Kozu is a fearsome warrior, with scary glowing green eyes. Under Lord Garmadon's orders, Kozu and his warriors built an unbeatable battle machine. Known as the Garmatron, it fired special Dark Matter missiles, infecting Ninjago City with evil energy.

The Stone Army seemed unbeatable, until the ninja's friend Dareth found a special helmet. When Dareth put it on, it gave him control of the Stone Army. He ordered the army to stop attacking Ninjago Island, and it obeyed. Easy!

Master Chen, owner of the Mr. Chen's Noodle House restaurant chain, seems like an ordinary businessman, but he's not. He's a vain and wicked man who wants to take over Ninjago Island and turn everyone into members of the Anacondrai tribe. Chen is also a Ninja Master. He trained Lord Garmadon after he became evil and also the cunning Clouse, who later became Chen's second-in-command.

Over the years, Chen has come up with many different plans to take over Ninjago Island, but

Chen

they have all failed. His most recent plan involved staging a Tournament of Elements. He invited all the ninja to take part in the contest, and they thought it sounded like fun. However, Chen's true plan was to steal their elemental powers. He hoped to use their combined powers to cast a spell that would turn everyone into Anacondrai.

Garmadon, Chen's former pupil, helped the ninja to thwart the plan and banish Chen to the Cursed Realm. Unfortunately, Clouse managed to escape and swore to get his revenge on the ninja.

Clouse

Master Wu's former pupil, Morro, was the Master of Wind, but he dreamed of becoming the Green Ninja. Unfortunately, it wasn't his destiny, so Morro ran away. His spirit traveled to the Cursed Realm, the home of lost and evil souls.

Morro's spirit grew bitter and angry. He still wanted to be the Green Ninja, so he escaped from the Cursed Realm and took possession of the true Green Ninja, Lloyd. Morro then released some of his ghostly companions from the Cursed Realm to help him take over Ninjago Island. These included Soul Archer, a supernatural archer who never misses; Bansha, a screaming sorceress with the power to control people's minds; Ghoultar, a not-so-smart spook who's scarily strong; and Wrayth, a grisly ghost biker.

The ninja's usual weapons were useless against the sneaky spooks, but they were able to fight them with some new ghost-busting weapons, Aeroblades. Then, Nya defeated them once and for all when she unlocked her True Potential and used her powers to create a tidal wave that wiped out the Cursed Realm.

GREATEST BATTLES

Every enemy brings different challenges for the ninja. However, thanks to Wu's training, the brave heroes always find a way to defeat their foes.

GETTING THROUGH TO GARMADON

For a while, Lord Garmadon was a seemingly unbeatable foe. However, the Green Ninja found a way to unlock the good guy within, transforming him from foe to friend.

SNEAKY SKELETON ARMY

Under the command of Lord Garmadon, this bony battalion tried to steal the Golden Weapons. They were ruthless, but mostly very stupid, so the ninja managed to outwit them.

SLIMY SERPENTINE TRIBES

The Serpentine were powerful enemies but often fought among themselves, instead of working together. They were no match for the ninja's teamwork.

ANCIENT STONE ARMY

The Stone Army appeared indestructible, until the ninja's friend Dareth used his head. He found the Army's fatal weakness—whoever wore a special helmet could control them.

NASTY NINDROIDS

The Digital Overlord programmed the Nindroids to attack Ninjago City. However, the ninja were able to defeat them using their high-tech weapons, the Techno-Blades.

CHEN AND CLOUSE

Chen and Clouse's love of the Anacondrai was their downfall. With Garmadon's help, the ninja used the Serpentine to trap them in the Cursed Realm.

GHOST WARRIORS

When Nya unlocked her True Potential, her new powers created a huge tidal wave that wiped out the Cursed Realm and its inhabitants, including Morro and his ghosts.

New Challenges

    The ninja have famously faced and defeated many evil foes. However, their many heroic acts have brought a surprising new challenge—fame! The team's defeat of the ghostly Morro really caught the attention of the good folk of Ninjago Island. Now, the public love them.

    Everyone wants to find out more about their favorite heroes, and the ninja have become

celebrities. People want to interview them, take photographs of them, hire them for ads—and they have even been made into action figures! The ninja have hired an agent, their old friend Dareth, to help them meet the demands of the public, but Dareth is determined to turn them into even bigger celebrities. Kai loves being famous, but not all of the ninja do—Lloyd just wants to focus on being a ninja. Will the team be able cope with life in the spotlight?

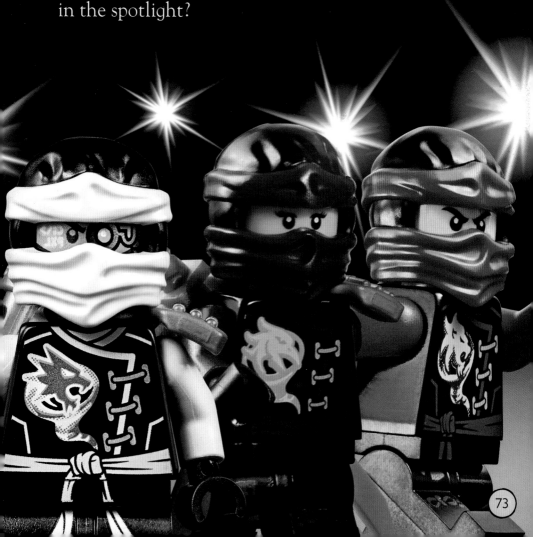

NINJA LIFE

Q: Kai, what is the best thing about being famous?
Kai: Being famous is awesome! I love that people know who we are and are interested in what we do. I want to be a good role model for our fans. And have you seen my action figure? It's so cool!

Q: Cole and Zane, do you ever feel different than the rest of the ninja?
Cole: Do you mean because I'm a ghost and he's a Nindroid? No way! We're a team and we all work together. We're all different—that's what makes us so special.

Q: Nya, how does it feel to be the only female on the team?
Nya: I don't really think about it. I just work hard and try to be the best ninja I can. I'm just as good as the boys at everything I do!

Q: Lloyd, what does the future hold for the Green Ninja?
Lloyd: My dream is to train future ninja, like Master Wu. I'd like to find the next generation of heroes. I want to make sure that the Ninjago world is always protected from evil forces.

On their days off, the ninja like to relax at home with their friend and agent, Dareth, and their trainers, Misako and Master Wu.

Getting used to being famous isn't the only challenge the ninja have to face. They also have a new foe, Nadakhan, to defeat. A magical being known as a Djinn, Nadakhan has the power to grant wishes. That sounds fantastic, but it really isn't. Nadakhan is so evil that he twists the wisher's words until they mean something totally different. Most people end up wishing that they hadn't wished for anything at all!

Nadakhan is actually a prince from a magical realm called Djinjago. However, he is more famous for being captain of a ship, called *Misfortune's Keep*, and commander of its pirate crew. Many years ago Nadakhan was captured and trapped in the mysterious Teapot of Tyrahn. However, he recently escaped when the Teapot was found. Once free, he discovered that his home world had been lost when the ninja destroyed the Cursed Realm. Although it was an accident, Nadakhan is determined to make the ninja pay for what they did.

NADAKHAN'S EVIL PLAN

I have spent many years trapped in the Teapot of Tyrahn. Now that I am free, I have come up with a plan to regain my rightful place as the ruler of Djinjago. I believe it is my most cunning plan yet.

1 First, I will reassemble my pirate crew and rebuild my ship, *Misfortune's Keep*.

2 Those dratted ninja destroyed Djinjago with their meddling. I will take revenge on them by trapping their souls inside my Djinn Blade.

3 The girl Ninja, Nya, looks just like my lost love, Delara. Once I have captured her, I will marry her and become a djinn King!

4 Once I am a djinn King, I will have unlimited wishes, and then I will be truly unstoppable!

5 I will then rebuild my home world of Djinjago. Nya and I will rule over Djinjago together.

Nadakhan can't wait to carry out his evil plan. His first move is to go and find his old crew.

First-mate Flintlocke is as loyal as any pirate can be, while pirate Dogshank is so strong that she uses the ship's anchor as a weapon. Gold-loving Doubloon prefers fighting to talking, while Cyren is the opposite—she sings her enemies into a trance. Mechanical mechanic Monkey Wretch makes sure that *Misfortune's Keep* is in perfect working order, while peg-legged Clancee keeps the decks spick-and-span with his mop. Nadakhan also finds two new recruits, named Landon and Colin. Nadakhan doesn't think these are good names for pirates, so he names them Bucko and Sqiffy instead.

Over the years, *Misfortune's Keep* has become a wreck, so Nadakhan and his crew have to repair it. They add an awesome new feature—flight—and Nadakhan renames his crew the Sky Pirates.

Dogshank

Monkey Wretch

Clancee

Bucko

Flintlocke

Doubloon

Cyren

Sqiffy

MISFORTUNE'S KEEP

While Nadakhan was imprisoned in the Teapot of Tyrahn, his ship *Misfortune's Keep* became a bit of a wreck. However, when he was released, Nadakhan and his pirate crew worked hard to fix it up. Now, it's better than ever, with lots of sneaky new features.

WALK THE PLANK!
Like any good pirate ship, *Misfortune's Keep* has a plank for enemies to walk off.

PIRATE JET
Instead of a lifeboat, the ship has a detachable jet that can zoom off on separate missions.

PIRATE FLAG
Nadakhan lets everyone know pirates are coming with his menacing pirate flag.

MAIN WEAPON
The ship's firepower includes a powerful double-barrelled cannon.

SECRET WEAPONS
The twin engines also have small hidden cannons.

FLYING SHIP
Nadakhan added twin propellers to enable the ship to fly.

Nadakhan has captured Nya and taken her back to *Misfortune's Keep*. He gives Cyren and Monkey Wretch the task of guarding Nya to make sure she doesn't escape.

Jay knows he must act fast to rescue Nya. Brave Jay clears his mind of fear to summon some lightning-fast transportation—his Elemental Dragon. The speedy dragon flies him toward *Misfortune's Keep* in a flash.

When Cyren and Monkey Wretch see Jay approaching, they take off in their flyer to meet Jay in midair. Monkey Wretch takes aim with a harpoon gun, but the dragon easily dodges the harpoons. The dragon fights back by shooting lightning from its mouth, finally bringing down the flyer. With Cyren and Monkey Wretch out of the way, Jay flies the Elemental Dragon over to *Misfortune's Keep* to find Nya.

Jay sneaks on board *Misfortune's Keep* disguised
as a pirate and frees Nya. But they still have
Nadakhan to deal with. Jay and Nya battle
bravely, but Nadakhan is too powerful. Just when
it looks like the dastardly djinn will defeat them,
the rest of the team arrive! Nadakhan is no match
for a team of ninja working together, and the
ninja manage to escape.

The ninja have foiled Nadakhan's evil plot, and Ninjago Island is safe again—for now. Nadakhan is still determined to get his revenge on the ninja, but the heroes know that whatever challenges the future may bring, they will be able to face them as a team. In the meantime, they can celebrate their latest victory with a well-earned cup of tea back in Ninjago City.

WHICH NINJA ARE YOU?

The ninja are a strong and loyal team of heroes, but they all have different personalities and strengths. Answer the questions to see which ninja you are most like.

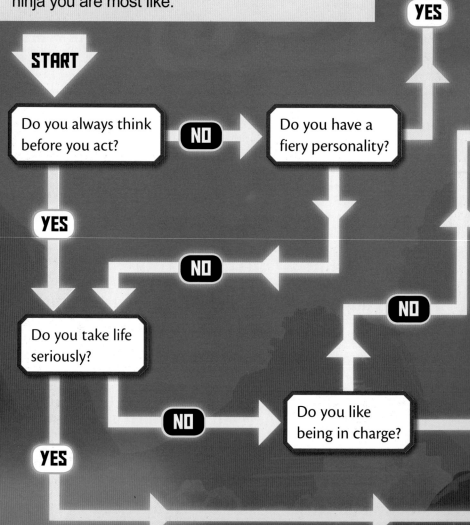

START

Do you always think before you act?

NO → Do you have a fiery personality?

YES

YES

NO

NO

Do you take life seriously?

Do you like being in charge?

NO

YES

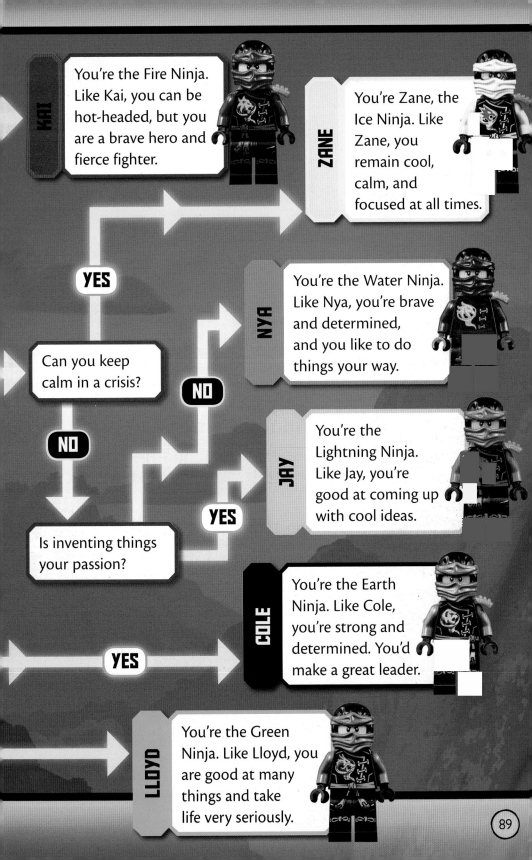

KAI — You're the Fire Ninja. Like Kai, you can be hot-headed, but you are a brave hero and fierce fighter.

ZANE — You're Zane, the Ice Ninja. Like Zane, you remain cool, calm, and focused at all times.

YES

Can you keep calm in a crisis?

NO

NYA — You're the Water Ninja. Like Nya, you're brave and determined, and you like to do things your way.

NO

JAY — You're the Lightning Ninja. Like Jay, you're good at coming up with cool ideas.

Is inventing things your passion?

YES

COLE — You're the Earth Ninja. Like Cole, you're strong and determined. You'd make a great leader.

YES

LLOYD — You're the Green Ninja. Like Lloyd, you are good at many things and take life very seriously.

Quiz

1. What was Jay doing when Master Wu first met him?

2. What is Nya's element?

3. Where does Cole get turned into a ghost?

4. What is the name of the scientist who created Zane?

5. Which ninja usually wears blue?

6. What is Ninjago Island's largest city?

7. Which status do the ninja have to reach in order to get dragon robes?

8. What does Kai name his dragon?

9. Which Serpentine tribe does Pythor belong to?

10. What special, high-tech weapons do the ninja use to defeat the Nindroids?

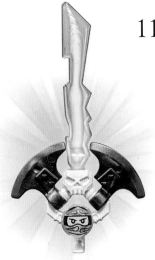

11. Morro was the master of which element?

12. Who do the ninja hire as their agent?

13. What does Nadakhan name his crew?

14. Where does Nadakhan keep Nya captive?

15. What does Jay summon in order to fly to Nadakhan's ship?

Answers on page 93

Glossary

Acquire
Gain possession of something

Agile
Graceful and light on one's feet

Archaeologist
Someone who studies ancient objects

Consequence
The result of a particular event or action

Cunning
Clever and sneaky

Dastardly
Mean and cruel

Discipline
Self-control

Dratted
Pesky or annoying

Enroll
Become a member of an organization, such as a school

High-tech
Made from the latest technology

Inhabitants
The people who live in a certain place

Kendo
A martial art in which the participants use swords and wear protective armor

Marauding
Causing trouble

Nunchuks
A weapon consisting of
two sticks on a chain

Peak
The highest point of
a mountain

Phantom
Ghost

Scythe
A weapon with a
sharp, curved blade

Shuriken
A star-shaped weapon
that is designed to be
thrown

Stealthily
Quietly and secretively

Summon
Make appear

Supernatural
To do with ghosts

Thwart
Stop or defeat someone
or something

Tornado
A type of storm formed
of spinning air

Tranquility
Peacefulness

Trident
A sword with three
prongs

Wield
Hold or use a weapon

Answers to the quiz on pages 90 and 91:
1. Testing a pair of mechanical wings 2. Water 3. The Temple of
Airjitzu 4. Dr Julien 5. Jay 6. Ninjago City 7. DX status 8. Flame
9. The Anacondrai 10. Techno-Blades 11. Wind 12. Dareth
13. The Sky Pirates 14. *Misfortune's Keep* 15. His Elemental Dragon

Guide for Parents

This book is part of an exciting four-level reading series for children, developing the habit of reading widely for both pleasure and information. These chapter books have a compelling main narrative to suit your child's reading ability. Each book is designed to develop your child's reading skills, fluency, grammar awareness, and comprehension in order to build confidence and engagement when reading.

Ready for a Level 4 book

YOUR CHILD SHOULD

- be able to read independently and silently for extended periods of time.
- read aloud flexibly and fluently, in expressive phrases with the listener in mind.
- be able to respond to what is being read and be able to discuss key ideas in the text.

A VALUABLE AND SHARED READING EXPERIENCE

Supporting children when they are reading proficiently can encourage them to value reading and to view reading as an interesting, purposeful, and enjoyable pastime. So here are a few tips on how to use this book with your child.

TIP 1 Reading aloud as a learning opportunity:
- after your child has read a part of the book, ask him/her to tell you what has happened so far.
- even though your child may be reading independently, most children at this level still enjoy having a parent read aloud. Take turns reading sections of the book, especially sections that contain dialogue that can provide practice in expressive reading.

TIP 2 Praise, share, and chat:

- encourage your child to recall specific details after each chapter.
- provide opportunities for your child to pick out interesting words and discuss what they mean.
- talk about what each of you found most interesting or most important.
- ask the questions provided in the quiz at the back of the book. These help to develop comprehension skills and awareness of the language used.
- ask if there's anything that your child would like to discover more about.

Further information can be researched in the index of other non-fiction books or on the Internet.

A FEW ADDITIONAL TIPS

- Continue to read to your child regularly to demonstrate fluency, phrasing, and expression; to find out or check information; and for sharing enjoyment.
- Encourage your child to read a range of different genres, such as newspapers, poems, review articles, and instructions.
- Provide opportunities for your child to read to a variety of eager listeners, such as a sibling or a grandparent.

Series consultant, **Dr. Linda Gambrell**, Distinguished Professor of Education at Clemson University, has served as President of the National Reading Conference, the College Reading Association, and the International Reading Association.

Index